Why do we remember?

REMEMBRANCE DAY

Izzi Howell

W
FRANKLIN WATTS
LONDON · SYDNEY

Franklin Watts
First published in Great Britain in 2016 by The Watts Publishing Group
Copyright © The Watts Publishing Group, 2016

Produced for Franklin Watts by
White-Thomson Publishing Ltd
www.wtpub.co.uk

ISBN: 978 1 4451 4847 2

Credits
Series Editor: Izzi Howell
Series Designer: Rocket Design (East Anglia) Ltd
Designer: Clare Nicholas
Series Consultant: Philip Parker

The publisher would like to thank the following for permission to reproduce their pictures: Alamy/Lordprice Collection 7 (centre); Alamy/World History Archive 11 (bottom); Alamy/John Frost Newspapers 15; Alamy/Military Images 19; Alamy/Jenny Matthews 20; Alamy/keith morris 23 (centre); Alamy/Mar Photographics 24; Corbis/Bettmann 13; Corbis/ANDY RAIN/epa 27 (left); iStock/wcjohnston 2, 4; iStock/MarkSpowart 5; iStock/pamspix 28 (bottom); iStock/Catherine Lane 29; Mary Evans/ Illustrated London News Ltd 17; Shutterstock/wickerwood(title page and cover left); Shutterstock/Jan Holm (cover right); Shutterstock/Everett Historical 7 (left and centre), 8, 9, 10, 11 (top), 14 (bottom), 16 (top and bottom), 18; Shutterstock/Daniel Leppens 12; Shutterstock/Elzbieta Sekowska 14 (top); Shutterstock/Clive Chilvers 21; Shutterstock/RubinowaDama 22; Shutterstock/chrisbrignell (left and right); Shutterstock/Doug Schnurr 25; Shutterstock/Nadezda Zavitaeva 26; Shutterstock/chrisdorney 27 (right); Shutterstock/GTS Productions 28 (top).
All design elements from Shutterstock.

Every attempt has been made to clear copyright. Should there be any inadvertent omission please apply to the publisher for rectification.

Printed in China

MIX
Paper from
responsible sources
FSC® C104740
www.fsc.org

Franklin Watts
An imprint of
Hachette Children's Group
Part of The Watts Publishing Group
Carmelite House
50 Victoria Embankment
London EC4Y 0DZ

An Hachette UK Company
www.hachette.co.uk
www.franklinwatts.co.uk

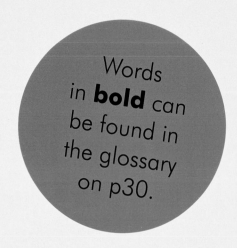

Words in **bold** can be found in the glossary on p30.

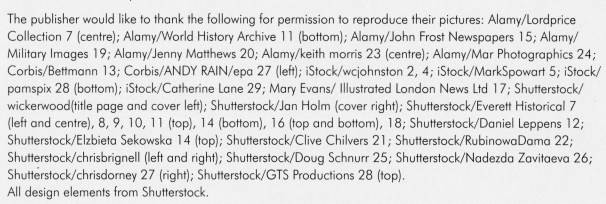

"At the going down of the sun and in the morning We will remember them."
Ode of Remembrance
(from For the Fallen - Laurence Binyon)

CONTENTS

WHAT IS REMEMBRANCE DAY?

Every year on Remembrance Day, people all over the world remember those who have been injured and killed in wars. In most **Commonwealth** countries, Remembrance Day takes place on 11 November because the First World War ended on that date in 1918.

Remembrance Day services are also held on the nearest Sunday to 11 November, which is known as Remembrance Sunday.

▼ At Remembrance Day services, people often lay **wreaths** of poppies. Poppies are a **symbol** of Remembrance Day.

4

HOW do we know?

You can learn more about Remembrance Day by going to a service in your local area on 11 November or Remembrance Sunday.

November 11

WHAT do you think?

Have you **observed** Remembrance Day before? What did you do?

▼ Remembrance Day is observed in many countries. This service is in Canada.

THE FIRST WORLD WAR

The story of Remembrance Day started over a hundred years ago in 1914, when a war about land and power started in Europe. In the beginning, Germany and **Austria-Hungary** fought against the UK, France and Russia. Later, as more countries joined in, this war became known as the First World War.

▲ This map shows the countries that fought at the beginning of the First World War.

FIND OUT FOR YOURSELF
Whose murder was the cause of the First World War?

In 1914, most people in the UK thought that the war would finish by the end of the year. The government encouraged young men to join the army. After seeing their friends go off to war, many young men decided to join the army. They thought that it would be an exciting adventure.

HOW do we know?

We can look at posters from 1914 that were made to encourage young men to join the army.

▲ These posters were put on buses and public buildings so that many people would see them.

WHAT do you think?

Why do you think men wanted to join the army after seeing posters like these?

LIFE IN THE TRENCHES

Many battles in the First World War were fought in France and Belgium. Soldiers from both sides lived in **trenches** close to the battlefields. The trenches were cold, muddy and full of rats.

▼ Piles of sandbags supported the walls of the trenches.

The land between the trenches was called **No Man's Land**, because it didn't belong to either side. Soldiers crossed No Man's Land to fight the enemy and try to take over their trenches. In these attacks, many men were hurt or killed by bombs, bullets and **poison gas**. Many others were taken prisoner.

▼ No Man's Land was covered in water-filled shell holes and dead trees.

HOW do we know?

Many soldiers kept diaries of their experiences in the trenches.

WHAT do you think?

How do you think the soldiers felt in the trenches? How do you think they felt when they went into No Man's Land?

66 The trenches are ankle deep – some places calf deep – in mud ... the men are wet through. 99

Captain Charlie May, 29 November 1915

SIGNING THE ARMISTICE

In April 1917, the USA joined Britain and its **allies**. They sent many soldiers to fight in the trenches. Soon, Germany and its allies realised that they couldn't win the war. They had lost too many of their soldiers, and the other side was stronger.

In November 1918, Germany **surrendered**. They signed an armistice — a **document** that said that they wouldn't fight any more. The First World War ended at 11 a.m. on 11 November 1918.

Read all about it!

▲ News of Germany's surrender was on the front pages of newspapers around the world.

▶ Crowds of people gathered in London to celebrate the end of the First World War.

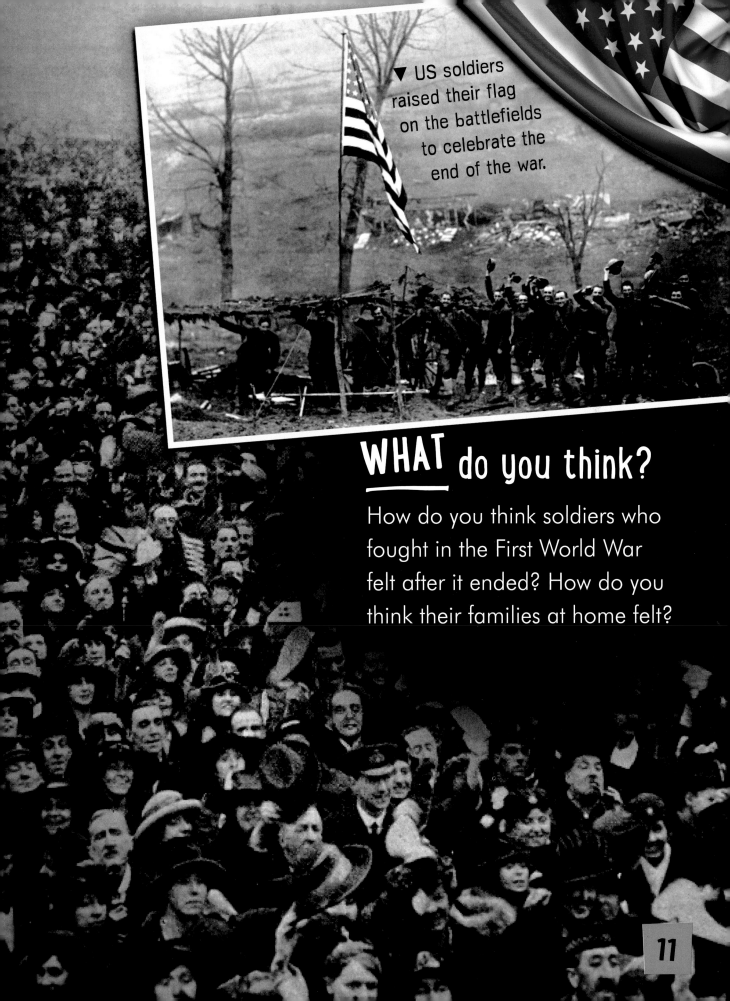

▼ US soldiers raised their flag on the battlefields to celebrate the end of the war.

WHAT do you think?

How do you think soldiers who fought in the First World War felt after it ended? How do you think their families at home felt?

AFTER THE FIRST WORLD WAR

Over 8.5 million soldiers died in the First World War. Many men were buried in **cemeteries** close to the battlefields in France and Belgium. A group called the Commonwealth War Graves Commission (CWGC) looks after many of these cemeteries.

▲ These British gravestones are in a French cemetery.

WHAT do you think?

Why is it important to look after cemeteries?

Although the First World War was a very difficult, sad time, people didn't want to forget about it. They began to hold remembrance services every year on 11 November to honour the soldiers who had died or been injured. This day became known as Armistice Day.

▼ This photo shows the Armistice Day **procession** in London in 1925.

THE SECOND WORLD WAR

After the First World War, people hoped that there would never be another world war. Sadly, the peace didn't last long.

In the 1930s, a **political party** called the Nazis took charge in Germany. They wanted Germany to be the strongest country in Europe. In 1939, Germany **invaded** nearby Poland. Britain and France went to war with Germany, and many other countries quickly joined in. Russia became an ally of Britain, and Italy and Japan joined the German side.

◄ Adolf Hitler (1889–1945) was the leader of the Nazi party.

► The German army invading Poland in September 1939.

SUNDAY EXPRESS, SEPTEMBER 3, 1939.

SPECIAL
WAR
EDITION

Sunday Express

HE PAPER THAT IS DIFFERENT

4 P.M.

Registered at the G.P.O.
As a newspaper.

JOHANNESBURG, SEPTEMBER 3, 1939.

THREEPENCE.

STOP PRESS
NEWS
PAGE 4

WAR DECLARED ON GERMANY

Britain's Ultimatum Ignored By Hitler

FRANCE WILL FIGHT TOO, CHAMBERLAIN TELLS EMPIRE

Mr. Neville Chamberlain

How the Premier Told the Empire

LIKE hundreds of thousands of people throughout the Empire, I choked with emotion when I heard Mr. Neville Cham-

LONDON, Sunday.

THE WHOLE BRITISH EMPIRE HEARD THE DIGNIFIED ANNOUNCEMENT AT 12.15 (SOUTH AFRICAN TIME) TO-DAY BY MR. NEVILLE CHAMBERLAIN, PRIME MINISTER OF GREAT BRITAIN, THAT BRITAIN WAS AT WAR WITH GERMANY.

Mr. Chamberlain announced in the House of Commons that France had joined Great Britain in the war against Germany.

AT 12.15 (SOUTH AFRICAN TIME) MR. CHAMBERLAIN SPOKE ON THE RADIO FROM No. 10 DOWNING STREET TO THE WHOLE EMPIRE.

The British Premier's voice was steady and firm as he said: "This country is at war with Germany."

MILLIONS OF LISTENERS WERE OVERCOME WITH EMOTION AS MR. CHAMBERLAIN, IN THE MOST MOMENTOUS SPEECH EVER MADE BY A BRITISH PREMIER, SAID: "WE HAVE A CLEAR CONSCIENCE."

There was a hush throughout the British Empire as Mr. Chamberlain concluded his speech.

He said with moving sincerity in a deep voice, "God bless you all."

AN APPEAL WAS MADE TO PAY PARTICULAR ATTENTION TO THE REQUESTS MADE BY THE AUTHORITIES.

Mr. Chamberlain's Speech

Mr. Chamberlain's speech was as follows:

"I am speaking to you from the Cabinet room of 10 Downing Street. This morning the British Ambassador in Berlin handed the German Government the final Note stating that unless we heard from them by eleven o'clock that they were prepared at once to withdraw their troops from Poland, a state of war would exist between us.

broadcast on Thursday night, Hitler did not wait to hear any comments on them but ordered his troops to cross the Polish frontier the next morning.

"His action shows convincingly that there is no chance of expecting that this man will ever give up his intention of using force to gain his will. He can only be stopped by force.

"We and France are to-day going, in fulfilment of our obligations, going to the aid of Poland so bravely resisting this wicked and unprovoked attack upon her people.

We have a clear Conscience

"We have a clear conscience. We have done all that any country could have done to establish peace. The situation, however, in which no word given by Germany's ruler could be trusted and no people nor country can feel itself safe has become intolerable.

"And now we have resolved to finish it.

"I know that you will all play your part with calmness and courage.

"At such a moment as this, the assurances of support we have received from the Empire are a source of profound encourage-

HIS MAJESTY THE KING

BRITISH PREMIER EXPLAINS

THE BRITISH PREMIER WAS LOUDLY CHEERED WHEN PARLIAMENT MET AT NOON. MR. CHAMBERLAIN ROSE IMMEDIATELY TO DECLARE A STATE OF WAR WITH GERMANY.

Greeted with loud cheers, Mr. Chamberlain said: When I spoke last night to the House I could not but be aware that in some parts of the House there was bewilderment as to whether...

HOW do we know?

We can see when Britain started fighting in the Second World War from newspapers that were printed all over the world at that time.

FIND OUT FOR YOURSELF
In the Second World War, which countries were known as the Allies?

BATTLES AND BOMBS

Battles in the Second World War were fought on land, at sea and in the air. The fighting took place in Europe, Asia and Africa.

◄ Both sides used **torpedoes** to attack enemy ships carrying weapons, soldiers and supplies.

As well as the soldiers who fought in the battles, many ordinary people were hurt in the Second World War. Both sides dropped bombs on towns and cities. The Nazis killed millions of people in the countries that they controlled, particularly **Jewish** people.

▲ German planes dropped bombs on many British cities, such as London. These attacks were called air raids.

▼ Bombs and rockets destroyed buildings and houses in Coventry, England. Many people died in air raids.

HOW do we know?

Many people still remember what it was like to experience an air raid.

> **"Explosions like volcanoes, the sky turning black, livid red, billowing smoke – I thought the sky was falling in – the noise was deafening."**
>
> Brenda McColl
> (an air raid survivor from London)

THE END OF THE SECOND WORLD WAR

By 1943, Britain and its allies were starting to win the war. When Germany surrendered in 1945, the fighting in Europe finished.

However, there were still battles between the USA and Japan until the USA dropped **atomic bombs** on two cities in Japan in August 1945. The bombs did so much damage that Japan surrendered. The Second World War was finally over.

◀ The cloud made by the atomic bomb dropped on the city of Nagasaki, Japan.

FIND OUT FOR YOURSELF What does VE stand for?

Yippee, it's all over!

<u>HOW</u> do we know?

We can see photographs taken during and after the end of the Second World War.

▲ People celebrating the end of the Second World War in London on VE Day.

19

SILENT REMEMBRANCE

After the Second World War, the name 'Armistice Day' was changed to 'Remembrance Day'. This was to **commemorate** soldiers from both world wars who had lost their lives.

Today, most Remembrance Day and Remembrance Sunday services include two minutes of silence at 11 a.m. On both days, people gather together to remember those who have died **in action** and give thanks to them.

▲ These schoolchildren are taking part in two minutes of silence during a Remembrance Day service.

WHAT do you think?

What do you think people think about during the two minutes' silence?

◄ Before the minutes of silence, a bugler often plays the 'Last Post', a **traditional** piece of music from Commonwealth army funerals.

► This section of the poem *'For the Fallen'* is often read at Remembrance Day services.

They shall grow not old,
as we that are left grow old:
Age shall not weary them,
nor the years condemn.
At the going down of the
sun and in the morning
We will remember them.

Ode of Remembrance (from *For the Fallen* – Laurence Binyon)

POPPIES

After the First World War, some **veterans** started making and selling paper poppies to raise money for other soldiers. They were **inspired** by a poem about the poppies that grew on the battlefields of France after the war.

Paper poppies are still sold today. Many people wear poppies around Remembrance Day as a sign of **respect** for current soldiers and veterans. The money raised by selling poppies goes to help injured soldiers and the families of soldiers who have been killed.

▼ In 2014, the lawns of the Tower of London were filled with **ceramic** poppies to commemorate the **centenary** of the start of the First World War.

► This poppy seller collects **donations** in exchange for poppies.

Get your poppies here!

FIND OUT FOR YOURSELF Which charity sells paper poppies in the UK?

▲ Around 40 million poppies are made each year.

PLEASE HELP THE POPPY APPEAL

HOW do we know?

You can read about the Poppy Appeal online or see people in the UK selling poppies in public places in early November.

WHAT do you think?

Poppies are bright and beautiful flowers, but they don't live long. Why are they a good symbol of soldiers who fought in the First World War?

23

VETERANS

Today, Remembrance Day services commemorate soldiers who have been injured and killed in all wars, including the recent wars in Iraq and Afghanistan.

◀ Veteran Rick Clement was injured by a bomb in Afghanistan in 2010, but has learned to walk again with the use of **prosthetic** legs. He is on his way to lay a wreath to commemorate those who have died in battle.

> " I ... pay my respects to all those that have lost their lives, from the friends I lost, to all of the people that have served their country. "
>
> Sergeant Rick Clement

Both young and old veterans attend Remembrance Day services. Sadly, no First World War veterans are alive today, but there are many veterans from the Second World War and other more recent wars.

▼ Veterans often wear uniforms to Remembrance Day services. This Canadian veteran received several medals during his time in the army.

HOW do we know?

Veterans give speeches at Remembrance Day services so that they can share their **eyewitness** experiences with others.

WHAT do you think?

Have you ever been an eyewitness to a big event? How do you think seeing an event is different to hearing about it?

MONUMENTS
AND MEMORIALS

After the First World War, it was hard for people to visit the graves of their family and friends, as most soldiers were buried in France and Belgium. Many towns in the UK built war **memorials** to remember those who were buried far away. The names of soldiers who lost their lives in the Second World War were added later.

Remembrance Day services usually take place at war memorials. In London, one of the largest services takes place at a monument called the Cenotaph.

◄ Here are the surnames and initials of some soldiers who died in the two world wars.

HOW do we know?

You can visit a war memorial in your local area, or the Cenotaph in London.

▶ Wreaths of poppies are placed on the Cenotaph.

▲ Queen Elizabeth II lays a poppy wreath at the Cenotaph on Remembrance Day.

WHAT do you think?

Why are war memorials a good way to remember those who died in wars? Can you think of some other ways to remember wars?

AROUND THE WORLD

▼ Australians lay poppy wreaths on Anzac Day.

Many countries that fought in the world wars observe Remembrance Day on 11 November and hold services on the nearest Sunday. In countries such as South Africa, they lay poppy wreaths and hold a silence to honour the dead.

Some countries hold services on different dates. In the USA, they observe Memorial Day on the last Monday in May. In Australia and New Zealand, they hold Anzac Day remembrance services on 25 April.

FIND OUT FOR YOURSELF
How did Anzac Day get its name?

◀ During the First World War, Anzac biscuits were sold in Australia and New Zealand to raise money for the soldiers fighting abroad. These biscuits are still eaten on Anzac Day today.

HOW do we know?

We can talk to people from different countries about how they remember war and those who lost their lives.

WHAT do you think?

How will you remember those who have died in wars? How could you observe Remembrance Day?

▼ Each of the soldiers marching in this Memorial Day parade is wearing a uniform from a different time period of the US army.

Hup, two, three, four!

GLOSSARY

allies – countries that have agreed to help one another in a war

atomic bomb – a very powerful bomb

Austria-Hungary – in the past, this was an empire ruled by one person, but today it is divided into many countries, such as Austria, Hungary and the Czech Republic.

barbed wire – strong wire with spikes on it

cemetery – a place where dead people are buried

centenary – the day or year that is one hundred years after an important event

ceramic – describes something made from clay that has been hardened by baking

commemorate – to do something to show you remember an important person or event with respect

Commonwealth – a group of countries including the UK, Australia and Canada, which have trade and cultural links. In the past, most Commonwealth countries were part of the British Empire.

document – a piece of paper with official information on it

donation – money that is given to help a group or a person

eyewitness – someone who sees an event happen

in action – while fighting in a war

inspire – to give someone an idea

invade – to enter a country in order to take control of it

Jewish – describes someone who follows the religion of Judaism

memorial – an object that is built to help people remember an imporant event

No Man's Land – an area of land in a war that no one controls

observe – to take part in a ceremony

poison gas – gas that can hurt or kill you if you breathe it in

political party – a political group that wants to be, or is, in charge of a country

procession – a line of people that moves together slowly as part of an event

prosthetic – describes a fake body part that replaces a missing part

respect – behaviour that shows you think that something is important

surrender – to stop fighting and admit that you have been beaten

symbol – something that is used to represent something else

torpedo – a bomb that is fired from a ship and moves under water to destroy another ship

traditional – describes something that has been done in the same way for a long time

trench – a long narrow hole dug in the ground for soldiers

veteran – someone who has been in the armed forces during a war

wreath – a large ring of leaves and flowers

TIMELINE

28 July 1914	The First World War begins.
11 Nov 1918	The First World War ends when Germany surrenders and signs an armistice.
11 Nov 1919	Armistice Day is celebrated for the first time.
1 Sept 1939	The Second World War begins when Germany invades Poland.
8 May 1945	Germany surrenders and the Second World War ends in Europe.
15 Aug 1945	The Second World War ends worldwide.
7 Oct 2001	The USA, the UK and other allies invade Afghanistan and begin fighting against its government.
20 March 2003	The USA, the UK and other allies invade Iraq and begin fighting against its government.
26 Oct 2014	American and UK soldiers leave Afghanistan.

INDEX